Spiritual Gardens

A Guide to Meditating in Nature

Danijela Kracun & Charles McFadden

Schiffer Publishing Ltd
4880 Lower Valley Road • Atglen, PA • 19310
Printed in China

Library of Congress Control Number: 2011920081

Designed by Danielle D. Farmer
Cover Design by Bruce Waters

Type set in University Roman BT/Chalet-LondonNineteenSeventy/ Chalet-NewYorkNineteenEighty

ISBN: 978-0-7643-3731-4
Printed in China

Schiffer Books are available at special discounts for bulk purchases for sales promotions or premiums. Special editions, including personalized covers, corporate imprints, and excerpts can be created in large quantities for special needs. For more information contact the publisher:

Published by Schiffer Publishing Ltd.
4880 Lower Valley Road
Atglen, PA 19310
Phone: (610) 593-1777; Fax: (610) 593-2002
E-mail: Info@schifferbooks.com

For the largest selection of fine reference books on this and related subjects, please visit our website at:
www.schifferbooks.com

We are always looking for people to write books on new and related subjects. If you have an idea for a book please contact us at the above address.

This book may be purchased from the publisher.
Include $5.00 for shipping.
Please try your bookstore first.
You may write for a free catalog.

In Europe, Schiffer books are distributed by
Bushwood Books
6 Marksbury Ave.
Kew Gardens
Surrey TW9 4JF England
Phone: 44 (0) 20 8392 8585; Fax: 44 (0) 20 8392 9876
E-mail: info@bushwoodbooks.co.uk
Website: www.bushwoodbooks.co.uk

CONTENTS

DEDICATION

"Dedicated and wishes of Peace and Love to
Tim, Sam, Tristan, Lucia, Cameron, Kordy, Baby Girl,
and all of the children of the world."

ACKNOWLEDGMENTS

Much thanks to our editor, Jennifer Marie Savage, the entire Schiffer Publishing team, and Jeff Allen for his photos and support.

What is a Spiritual Garden

INTRODUCTION

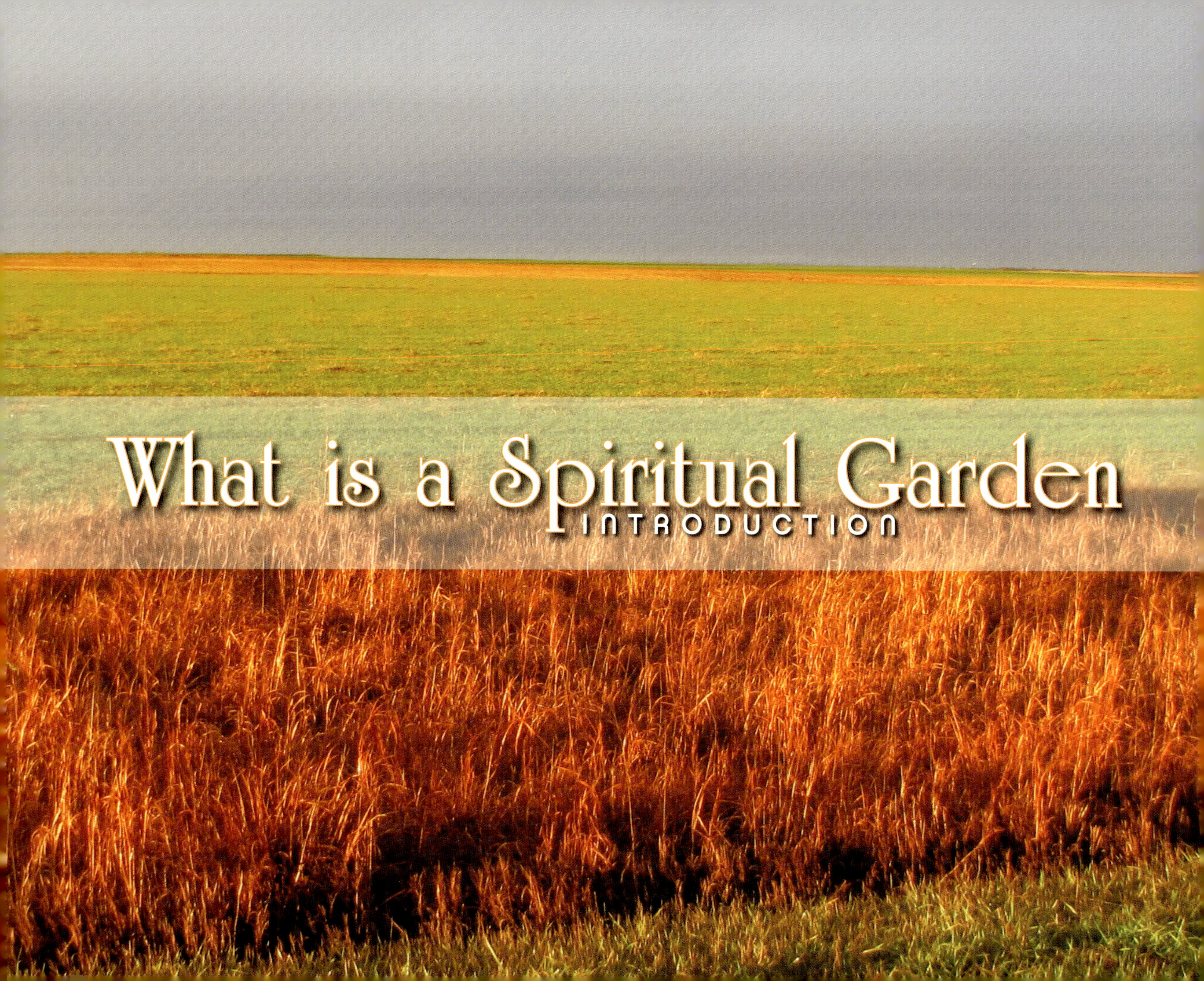

Bellingrath Gardens and Home, Theodore, Alabama.
One can almost smell the rose in this picture...

One of the things we have found in writing this book is that what traditionally makes a spiritual garden is not what I originally thought. The perfect amount of this or that, it's none of those things. In many cultures, and in society in general, spiritual or Zen gardens must have a particular type of tree and setting or surrounding with the proper amount of lighting, water, rocks, and flowers. Although all gardens require the bare necessities for survival such as water, soil, and sun, we have discovered that any setting has the ability to be titled a landscape for healing, meditation and growth.

We traveled through many parts of the United States to take pictures for this book, and one of the most important things that we have learned is that there is beauty in every city and state we visited. The peace and beauty that always surrounds us is most of the time taken for granted and overlooked as ordinary. By finding a peaceful, beautiful spot and meditating or contemplating there, you will begin to see and feel the natural beauty of places you normally would not and the peace that often accompanies it. As you relax in that setting, let the peace and beauty penetrate you. By doing this often, you will find it follows you and is always with you throughout life, growing deeper within you day by day.

OPPOSITE: Somewhere in Kansas.
The sky opened up after a rainy day. The natural lighting for this shot was beautiful and the picture does not do justice to the actual evening.

Every landscape and garden is spiritual and healing. It is up to you to experience your surroundings, relax, and feel comfort and security. Hopefully this book will inspire you to take the time to quiet yourself and to not only enjoy naturally beautiful places, but also start to relax wherever you are and enjoy life. In this day and age where stress may be at the forefront of your life, may we suggest that you take the time to smell the roses. It's free and well worth your time!

Bellingrath Gardens and Home, Theodore, Alabama.
Take a seat and rest in the present moment...

Lititz, Pennsylvania,
...and enjoy the bursting colors in contrast to the calm fall background.

Cathedral Rock, Sedona, Arizona.
Similar to meditation and the journey within, this mountain is not hard to climb, but it does take some effort. The view from the top, though, is wonderful and certainly worth it.

Homestead, Florida.
Stopping in a parking lot to get lunch the sky looked so vibrant blue it called out to be photographed.

HEALING TOOLS

In this book, you will be provided with many different meditation tools for healing and growth. In some meditations, you will be asked to sit still and do nothing. In others, you will be asked to be very active in the meditation. All of this is good and none of this is good. The only person that can decide which type of meditation is most useful is you. You may find that at a particular point in your life one type of meditation is best and at other times some other type. That is the way it is supposed to be.

Meditation is a journey. It's a journey of self-discovery. Many times you will find that in order to get to the still point of meditation in which you are just a witness, you must try all the others first. This type of living is a road less traveled — a road on which you are often times left to make your own decisions and not follow the person before you. There may be some pointers along the way, but more often than not you will have to go within and listen to your inner voice. Trusting yourself and listening to that inner voice is not always easy. We have not been taught to trust ourselves. Now you have been challenged to engage in trusting yourself and listening to the voice within by choosing which type of meditation is best for you. Remember, they all may be best and none of them may be best, but you are the only one who makes that decision.

Some of you may read these words and they may resonate well with you. Others may read these words and not feel any connection to them. That is okay. Sometimes you may need to put a book down for a season to come back to it with a renewed sense of vision, and sometimes you come back to it only to find out that you are still not ready to hear it. All of this is perfectly normal. What makes it perfectly so is the building of one's self-trust. Knowing what you need at the time you need it.

All of these tools of meditation are for you to experiment with, or not experiment with. Meditating and self-healing is not an easy task and you will be challenged along the way. Most people do not see this as the way to go and will most likely tell you that self-healing through meditation is impossible — and it's okay for them to say so. You have to remember to stay strong in your beliefs and trust your inner voice to tell you what is best for you. What is right for you may not be right for someone else. The path you choose to travel may not be the correct path for someone else. Realizing that you cannot force your opinion on others will make others not to force their opinion on you.

North Western New Mexico.
We felt the silence of the mountain deep within.

You can choose to read these words lightheartedly or you may choose to apply these teachings. Whichever you choose is the right choice because there is no wrong way to go about it. The wrong way is not trusting yourself and second-guessing what you decide. Look with the eyes of love and you will be looked at with eyes of love. Live with love and peace in your life — and that vibration will spread to others no matter how they choose to be.

WHAT MAKES A GARDEN?

I have thought a lot about what sort of landscape constitutes a "spiritual garden" for healing, meditation, and growth. I have traveled across the country and taken many photos of different types of landscapes and gardens — and I have found that all of them was a place for healing, meditation, and personal growth based on my mood at the time.

While visiting Ohio, I remember feeling quite excited about this journey. I had just come across a Rose garden. The garden was full of many varieties of beautiful roses. The day was a rainy one, drizzling on the roses and leaving a soft mist in the air and dew on the entire garden. I sat down and enjoyed this feeling of noticeable change. I had embarked on a journey for this new book and at the same time the Roses had embarked on a transformational journey themselves. The old buds were dying and new ones came to life. The season was changing: fall was here, so the garden wasn't blooming as it would

Sedona, Arizona.
Sunset in Cathedral Rock,

City of Rocks State Park, Deming, New Mexico.
Mother Earth's Zen garden.

have been during the spring or summer. The transformation had begun on so many levels — the Rose garden and myself. Yet, for that brief moment of sitting and being still with the roses and being at peace with myself, everything remained just as beautiful. The moment of change was very noticeable and the awareness of it bigger than life. The garden and I had no separation besides the physical and for that brief moment we had become one.

What a wonderful experience to be able to write about. Yet, no matter how hard I try, words cannot express the feelings I felt in all of the different places that I had visited. As you read this, you may be familiar with some of the places and landscapes I chose to write about and you most likely have had your own experiences while visiting them.

While in Arizona visiting the different vortexes, I had started to feel overwhelmed with this book project. I had climbed many different rocks in one day and had started to feel claustrophobic. The landscape itself made me feel as if I just couldn't get out, but get out of what? What was making me feel that way? I sat down on one of the rocks and meditated on it for a little while. My discovery was not one that will surprise you. I was feeling boxed and the landscape was a representation of this box. When I sat at the top of the rock and relaxed, I saw a beautiful sky and a full moon in daytime. I realized all that I had been projecting on the rock and the state of Arizona was within myself and once the realization came to the forefront it was gone.

These two examples of landscapes for healing, meditation, and growth are very different. What I was hoping to share is that any place can be used for these purposes. There is no reason to box an experience with a particular location. That is not to say that some may be preferable than others. Sure, one might prefer a garden to a landfill. My point is that even a landfill can invoke a spiritual transformation and leave a lasting feeling of noticeable change. The noticeable change will stay with you as the moment you were aware of something within yourself and that makes it a landscape for growth upon which you can mediate on and healing can begin.

At my old house I had the most beautiful rose bush that I took care of very well. Every time the roses needed trimming I took care of them. I had noticed that this was something I was good at. I decided to plant some more roses and care and consideration began with the others too. Cultivating something is an extraordinary metaphor for life. Taking care of the roses taught me how to take care of my life. Remove weeds as you would remove the clutter in your life. Cut the old buds so new ones can grow, as you would let go of old paradigms that no longer fit in your life.

If you were to ask my children what my favorite flower is, they will quickly tell you the dandelion. Though it's listed as a weed, in my opinion the dandelion is one of the most beautiful flowers. I love walking upon a grassy meadow full of dandelions. To me it is like seeing hundreds of suns. Traditionally, dandelions would probably not be placed in a spiritual or Zen garden. What makes a garden spiritual or Zen is the simplicity of a few rocks, some sand, and possibly water. I like this method as well. It is hard to title one landscape worthy of such a title and not the other. For all of these landscapes and gardens have the credibility to be titled a landscape for healing, meditation, and growth. Not one is better than the other or more spiritual or relaxing. It is up to you to make it such. For as I said previously, meditating at a landfill just may be the biggest growing experience of your life.

Sedona, Arizona.
Enjoy the soothing colors of the desert.

Sacred Space
Chapter One

On the Road in Arizona.
The openness of this scene reminds us of the vastness we have within ourselves.

The sacredness of space exists in all of life. There is space in building a building, constructing a playground, and designing a garden. In all of this space, we come to realize, or compare, that if we need space for all the man-made materialistic endeavors, so to do we need the space in our minds. The playground designs have to be just right for the distance of a swing to swing, the opening of doors in buildings, and the planting of plants to allow for the proper amount of room to grow in the sun. If we don't have enough space, we can't grow. Just for a moment stop and picture your body. What do you look like? What are you made of? Well, you are made up of atoms. What are atoms? Atoms are space. You are that which you see all around you as a necessity to grow, although, most of us do not know that at all. This necessity for growth is always there, yet we never stop and feel it.

See yourself lying in a grassy green field looking up at the sky. The sky is the most perfect blue without a cloud in sight. You are that space. Clouds may appear at times and block the blue sky, but the sky is always there, just like the essence of you, God, the Holy Spirit, or whatever you choose to call it. That space is always there — thoughts may appear like the clouds, but as long as we recognize them for what they truly are and not engage them we can rest comfortably in the space that is always there for us.

OPPOSITE: Gap, Pennsylvania.
There is nothing like sitting on the Earth and relaxing... This field of dandelions appears to be inviting us to do just that.

Northwestern New Mexico.
The journey that one takes to reach the snow top mountains begins with one foot step.

City of Rocks State Park, Deming, New Mexico.

Hey! There we are! Wait. Is that us or are they just shadows of us? Cool, huh? But we digress... An open mind is similar to a clear sky with nothing to obstruct it.

Saguaron National Park, Tucson, Arizona.

Sometimes meditation can be a rough road, but that first step is well worth taking.

Blue Ridge section of the Appalachian Mountains, Virginia.
We enjoyed the purple and green trees mixing together in this area.

Appalachian Mountains, Tennessee. The mist slowly clears as the sun rises.

CLEAR SKY MIND MEDITATION

(Accompanying images from across the U.S.)

Find a comfortable spot to sit down, relax, close your eyes, and take several natural breaths. Picture a clear blue sky in your mind. The sky is vast and infinite — there's not a cloud in sight, just the perfect blue.

Think of a problem that you are dealing with and place it in the clear sky. Notice all the space around the problem — the infinite emptiness compared to the smallness of the problem you placed within the infinite sky. Can you relate to the space around the problem you placed in the clear sky rather than the problem itself? Can you allow the problem to dissolve into the space and clarity of the blue sky? Be creative and experiment with this meditation. Never stress yourself out by thinking you are doing a meditation wrong or assuming you need to have a particular outcome. Always be kind and gentle to yourself while meditating and any meditation you do will have value.

Here's a metaphor about the mind: You can see your mind as a free, clear, vast, open, blue sky. Notice the clouds of thinking that come and go in this clear sky. Do not confuse yourself with thinking you are the clouds because you're not — you are the clear sky. The clear sky is always there whether the clouds of thinking are storming or subtle; just realize what the clouds are and fall back into the clearness of the sky. In other words, most people believe they are their thoughts and not the pure clear awareness the thoughts are arising from.

Look up at the sky when you need a reminder of how spacious your mind can be, and once things are settled a sole path will emerge.

The mind, like the sky, is open and spacious.

Sometimes the sky like the mind seems cluttered but the clear sky is still present and the unseen space holds everything.

As you begin to quiet yourself and look at the clutter it finally has a chance to clear.

Just like the clouds in the sky the thoughts disappear and the clear sky that is always there is once again revealed.

Flagler County River to Sea Preserve, Flagler, Florida.

It was nice to be greeted by this friendly visitor-fed turtle and, as this frog demonstrates, nothing can hide when you see clearly.

Lincoln Trail State Park, Marshall, Illinois.

The stillness of this lake allowed for a clear reflection.

Clear Reflection

When you come to a body of water, allow it to inspire you to clearly reflect upon your life. Notice how a clear body of water will clearly reflect the surroundings without discrimination. Become still and allow yourself to clearly look at what and how you are creating in life. What surrounds you in life now? Are you surrounded by peace, love and joy, or are you seeing stress and busyness reflected back to you? Sometimes we find that a reflection will show us something we may not be willing to face. Seeing clearly and noticing what your environment is reflecting back to you will give you a good indication of where your life is heading and may be helpful in showing you steps to take toward a new direction.

McKinney Falls State Park, Austin, Texas.
While sitting in meditation the puddle became still and the reflection of the tree became clear.

Ormond Beach, Florida.
At first we may be shocked at a situation before us, but if we walk through it with clarity we can see calm waters ahead.

The Dawes Arboretum, Newark, Ohio.
You can sense the calmness of the Zen garden in The Dawes Arboretum.

SITTING MEDITATION

You can do a seated meditation anywhere outside or inside. There really is no better or worse place to do it. There is a false belief that you need to find a quiet spot to meditate. This is not true. It is nice to have a quiet place, but if you practice meditation in a very noisy place you may eventually be able to calm yourself more deeply and easily by facing, and becoming one, with your surroundings. With that said, in the beginning it is probably helpful for most people to meditate in a quiet comfortable place.

Oglebay Park, Wheeling, West Virginia.
We enjoyed sitting and soaking in the fall colors of the park.

Doing a Sitting Meditation

Well, sit down and relax. You can close your eyes, but again some people choose not to. It may be helpful in the beginning to close your eyes so you are not distracted by your surroundings. Start to follow your breath. Allow yourself to become effortless. Stay aware of your breath and remain open and aware of what is arising inside of you. Meditation is not meant to stop you from thinking. You will think. Just simply be aware of your breath and of the thoughts that are arising without any judgment about them, let them come and go just like the clouds in the clear sky.

If you find you cannot focus on your breath because you are overwhelmed by your thoughts, you can add a word, affirmation, or count your breath. For example, while inhaling you can say to yourself "peace" and while exhaling you can say the word "love." Keep doing this and every time you find you have lost your awareness and are not repeating the words just gently come back to saying them once again. Never beat yourself up because you lost your awareness of the breath. The mind wanders, but this will help train it to stay focused. You can also make up affirmations to use as you inhale and exhale. Inhaling "I am free" and exhaling "I am light." Be creative. Choose affirmations that will help your current state of mind. The example of "I am free" and "I am light" would be good if you are very stressed.

If you do not want to say words or affirmations to yourself, then you can also simply count your breaths. Just start counting and every time you lose count due to the mind wandering simply start over. Counting is not to see how high you can get and is not a competition in any way. It is just a tool to lasso the mind and increase your awareness. You may find that at different times different techniques will work for you, so always be open to mixing it up, such as saying words, affirmations, or counting. Toward the end of your meditation allow some time where you simply stop the technique you are using and just rest in your awareness. Allow yourself to rest in the inner silence that you may have uncovered by your natural calmness brought on by the meditation. Not only will this help bring peace into your life, but it will also show you how your mind is working. When most people see how their minds are working, they begin to wonder who's in charge — them or their thoughts.

McKinney Falls State Park, Austin, Texas.
The soft light filters through the trees as the natural light of the mind filters through the thoughts.

Grand Canyon, Arizona.
The many branches and leaves of this tree provided us with shade on a hot day. The mind branches out and expands the more you quietly watch it.

The Dawes Arboretum, Newark, Ohio.
Sitting under a tree is great for healing, meditating, and growing.

Walking Meditations

CHAPTER TWO

Oglebay Park, Wheeling, West Virginia.
Allow your mind to relax as you do a walking meditation. Try not to name or comment on the things you are seeing and hearing. Be aware and truly experience each moment.

The most common objection people say in regards to why they can't meditate is either they are too busy, they can't concentrate, or they just don't have the time. One of my favorite ways to meditate is to do a walking meditation. Everywhere you go you are using your legs — to the store, your backyard, getting around your house — so why not use that time to meditate. A walking meditation is a simple way to calm the body and mind...to let go of emotions that need not be.

OPPOSITE: Bellingrath Gardens and Home, Theodore, Alabama.
The meditation path may seem short and narrow at first, but you may find that it's actually quite vast.

There are many different walking meditations at your disposal so why not give them a try and see which one works best for you. Walking meditations can be done anywhere: the park, beach, mountains, even around your own house. The point of a walking meditation is to follow your breath as you inhale and exhale, feeling your feet touch the earth as you walk.

Note: There are many books about walking meditation. Thich Nhat Hanh is a teacher and writer you may want to check out if you want to know more about walking meditation.

Chinese Garden of Friendship, Sydney Australia.
Enjoy the twists and turns of your walking path. *Photography by Jeff Allen.*

St. John Neumann R.C. Church, Mount Laurel, New Jersey.
There's always a light at the end of a tunnel... Or is there?

The Dawes Arboretum, Newark, Ohio.
Feel your feet and sense your inhale and exhale as you walk.

The Dawes Arboretum, Newark, Ohio.
Sometimes what seems to be a dead end becomes a kick toward a new beginning.

Flagler County River to Sea Preserve, Flagler, Florida.
You never know where the road will take you.

Oglebay Park, Wheeling, West Virginia.
Details reveal themselves as one becomes quiet and still.

Ormond Beach, Florida.
The lotus symbolizes enlightenment in Buddhism. The seed must grow from the mud and mucky water to finally break the surface and then blossom.

Seeing Walking Meditation

The beauty of all of our seasons comes through brilliantly in a seeing walking meditation. As you walk slowly, simply allow yourself to stop and look at all that is available to you. Look at the ground or the broken sidewalk. Stop and look at the trees and leaves. Watch the ocean and all the birds flying around trying to catch fish, or your own feet as they move you forward. Pay attention to the world and all its beauty: the clouds in the sky, the sun shining gently across the land, kids coming home from school, and the dogs being walked. Life slows down when you pay attention to it all, so go out there and walk! Smell some wild flowers and check out the dandelions. There is a lot to see and no need to rush or label what you are seeing.

On the Road in Kansas.
Enjoy the natural lighting of a beautiful sunset after the rain.

Bellingrath Gardens and Home, Theodore, Alabama.

This is a view from a boardwalk around a bayou... Remaining calm and aware you may be amazed at the sights and sounds you come across in life.

Grand Canyon, Arizona.
Walking meditations can be done anywhere. It can even be a mall or city street. It doesn't have to be as grand as the Grand Canyon but if you have the chance go for it!

Lititz, Pennsylvania.
Feel free to take a break to smell the flowers while on a walking meditation.

Oglebay Park, Wheeling, West Virginia.
Upon settling down, one notices the texture of the surroundings.

LISTENING WALKING MEDITATION

Another really good walking meditation is a listening walking meditation. As you walk in the park or along the beach or even a busy street, listen to the sounds around you. The sounds of the ocean, the birds, leaves rustling, horns blaring, traffic, the wind, white noise — anything your ear picks up — and simply walk peacefully. As you pay attention to the sounds, you will find yourself becoming one with the noises around you and at some point they may become such a major part of you that it all becomes a hush. When you get to that point, simply start anew and go back to listening. Allow yourself to hear all the available sounds. This is a great way to practice calming the mind chatter and bring you into the now.

Bellingrath Gardens and Home, Theodore, Alabama.
With mindfulness one will begin to notice all of the sounds that were missed due to the chatter of the mind.

Blue Springs State Park, Florida.
Upon first glance these birds look like ornaments on a tree.

Everglades, Florida.
Upon first glance these birds look like ornaments on a tree.

ABOVE: Bellingrath Gardens and Home, Theodore, Alabama.
Don't be alarmed if you hear a bee...When meditating in nature, the sounds are part of the experience.

Oglebay Park, Wheeling, West Virginia.
The repetition of an affirmation can help focus the mind and break through the years of harmful habits and conditioning.

Oglebay Park, Wheeling, West Virginia.
Affirmations can also be molded to help you deal with your struggles and bring you back to the present moment. There is no past or future...only the now.

AFFIRMATION WALKING MEDITATION

Affirmation is a good tool to get you over a hump you might be dealing with that for some reason you just can't seem to let go of. For instance, you might be upset about your mother criticizing you about something and you had a fight. Now your emotions are all stirred like a jar of shaken glitter and you prefer to settle them down. As you walk slowly, pay close attention to your breath and, as you inhale, say to yourself, "I am at peace." As you exhale, say the same affirmation: "I am at peace." Do this for the length of your walk and at some point you will see your thoughts and emotions creeping in — simply watch them, let them go, and return to your breath. As you do this, you will sense your body calming down considerably. Allow this calming to take place. Don't panic and think, "Wait, this is not supposed to happen! I am supposed to be upset!" That's just your ego trying to get in the way. Simply watch it, recognize it, let it go, and return to the breath.

Gap, Pennsylvania.
Upon driving by this dandelion field, the red barn caught our eye. The contrast in colors really make the barn stand out.

The affirmation walking meditation can be done with any affirmation you see fit or necessary. What you decide your affirmation to be is your own choice. Be creative! It could be "I love myself" or "I let go of all suffering" — anything that will keep you in the moment and help you get past your difficulty. It's easy to read about spirituality, but when it comes to applying it we tend to leave it inside the book. If you like the sound of a walking meditation, go out and apply it. Walk your thoughts about the present or past away and keep yourself in the present moment.

Ormond Beach, Florida.
Feel free to personalize an affirmation based on your mood or surroundings.

Oglebay Park, Wheeling, West Virginia.
The repetition of an affirmation can help focus the mind and break through the years of harmful habits and conditioning.

Nature of Spirit

CHAPTER THREE

North Western New Mexico.
This photograph is not an illusion, but it will set up the next set of pictures.

ILLUSIONS

Many times in life we are faced with a situation and we know exactly how to handle it. We may say to ourselves, "Yes, I know exactly what that is and I know exactly what to do." We are so certain of it — only to find out, no, we were wrong. Understanding and realizing that only a small percentage of our thoughts are worthy of listening to and are mostly gibberish is a difficult concept for most. The mind likes to play tricks on us, making us believe in something that is not factual.

While traveling through the white sands of New Mexico, this interplay of the mind became apparent in one particular photo where the mountain looked like a wave on the shore. What a great concept to play with! What this interplay does is remind us that our thoughts are not all that we are and in fact hinder our progression as individuals. So the next time when you are faced with a difficult situation and you KNOW exactly how to go about it, take a look at these photos again and ask yourself, "Where could my mind be tricking me? Where in this situation do I need to be more aware of an illusion that may be presented before me?"

We perceive nothing as it truly is. We — as well as our surroundings — are made up of atoms, which are mostly space, and yet we perceive everything, including ourselves, to be solid. Take your time in judging your reality and try to experience it more clearly. When your mind is still, you experience less confusion and have a better chance of seeing things as they are.

(These white sand images are from Alamogordo, New Mexico.)

A snowy road? Nope, it is the desert once again.

Breaking through illusion and seeing clearly reveals the unnoticed peace that has always been with you.

The monkey mind seems to always want to label and categorize things. This can lead to false assumptions and worthless judgments.

One begins to see things as they are from the clear awareness brought forth by meditation.

Can you allow your senses to be relaxed and experience the essence of an event rather than making the event into an opinion or concept?

Remaining still and attentive one can witness illusion and error easily which allows balance and correction to occur.

North Western New Mexico.
This landscape looks like a sandy beach with a foamy ocean wave, but it is actually a desert.

ONENESS MEDITATION

The inter-connectivity of all life can be seen in the accompanying images. When you look at these pictures, hopefully you will see wholeness. The interplay of man-made structures and nature can seem ugly to the observer, but if you can stand back and look at how all life is interconnected, you may begin to see through the "ugliness" and gain the perspective of everything being okay exactly as it is. This is not to say it cannot or should not be changed. It helps to not fight the present moment and stops the struggle with what is. When you fight with what is, you cause separation of yourself and reality. This is how we may become stressed, sick, depressed, or sad. By wanting reality to be other than it is, we cause ourselves suffering. Again, it is not to say you cannot change things. If you peacefully accept what is, you can move forward with peace and love and, in the process, change the "ugliness" effortlessly.

Most spiritual teachings and religions say that God or the Source of all things is omnipresent and that there is only oneness. These teachings help us to feel safe at all times and, realizing we cannot separate from God or the Source, not to take what we are experiencing so seriously.

Ormond Beach, Florida.
The muck and the flower are one in this picture. If not for the muck there would be no flower.

Hollywood Beach, Florida.
When oneness is realized one can meditate even in busy or noisy places.

On the Road in Indiana.
The power lines and man made structures are usually judged as being hard on the eye. In this photograph we feel everything blends together beautifully.

Taos, New Mexico.
These earth ships blending into the desert are fully self sustained and off the grid. Man and nature working together as one. A representation of oneness at its best.

Walnut Canyon, Flagstaff, Arizona.

Here we are looking out of an early "earth ship." The Walnut Canyon natives rarely left their homes. Due to their understanding of nature, the canyon provided all of their needs.

Taos, New Mexico, Earth Ships.
This photo has a surreal quality to it due to the heat creating a watery mirage.

Bellingrath Gardens and Home, Theodore, Alabama.
When looking at scenery try to experience it without habitual reactions, opinions and ideas about how it should be. Enjoy it as it is.

OPPOSITE & ABOVE: McKinney Falls State Park, Austin, Texas.
We are all interconnected in the web of life.

Gaining Your Oneness

This meditation is also known as metta meditation or loving kindness meditation. This meditation can show you how the natural oneness and harmony of the mind can be divided and disturbed by your automatic conditioned reactions and your thoughts.

When you do this meditation, you may find that your heart is open at times, like when you imagine yourself with a loved one, and closed and feeling restricted at other times, like when you imagine being with an enemy. This meditation shows you how much power your mind has and how it can make you feel a certain way. Your heart's natural state is open and relaxed, but at the thought of an enemy it tightens and closes. There is no one there with you causing your heart to do this during the mediation. It is your conditioned reaction to close your heart at the sight of an enemy, even if that enemy is only in your mind. The Buddha said this is like holding a hot coal. The only one you are hurting is yourself. By repeatedly closing our hearts and restricting our bodies we are slowly killing ourselves. Drop the hot coal and live with an open heart. The goal of this meditation is to help you relax and be able to eventually have an open heart even while facing a so-called enemy or someone you dislike. You will sense not only the oneness of your heart, but also start to notice the oneness of all beings.

On the Road in Kansas.
The imperfections of this photograph make it beautiful and perfect in its oneness.

1. Sit down in a comfortable position. Close your eyes and allow yourself to become as relaxed as you can. Take a few moments to calm yourself.

2. Bring your awareness to your heart. Let your awareness rest at your heart during the entire meditation. While aware of your heart, think of a loved one (could be anyone — your child, spouse, mother, father, friend). Hold the loved one in your mind's eye for a few minutes as you remain aware of your heart. Remain this way for several minutes.

3. Next, while still being aware of your heart, bring someone who is neutral to you, such as a bank teller, the mailman, or a store cashier, into your mind's eye. How does you heart feel? Let yourself be with this person in your mind for a few more minutes.

4. Then, while still being aware of your heart, bring someone who you dislike or consider an enemy into your mind's eye. How does your heart feel? Stay focused on this person for a few minutes.

5. Finally imagine all living beings are with you and letting your heart shine out love and peace in all directions to all of the beings. How does your heart feel? Stay with this visualization for a few more minutes and then relax quietly for a few minutes.

North Western New Mexico.
Atoms are not solid therefore we are not solid. The same stillness, space and consciousness that runs thro ugh my body also runs through and is shared by you and the two cows in this picture.

Earth Ships, Taos, New Mexico.
Man is realizing he can no longer be separated from nature and needs to work with it for his own survival.

The Dawes Arboretum, Newark, Ohio.
Realizing the interconnection of all things may help one to be relaxed where ever they are.

Bellingrath Gardens and Home, Theodore, Alabama.
It's hard to swim upstream. Give into the flow.

THE FLOW

If our mind becomes still, we can start to perceive the flow of life and sense how this flow is moving through the events of our life. When you sense the flow your life becomes effortless. You flow with the "waters" and the currents of your life as opposed to fighting them. If you feel you are not at the right job because you have headaches everyday and are mean to your family then you may want to quiet down and see if you are out of your life's flow. My guess would be it is. When we learn to flow we avoid illness, stress, anger and depression. It may not be that easy to follow the flow though. In this world of instant gratification and getting and doing everything faster and faster we can easily get lost from the flow. When the flow naturally slows down we have to have the patience to rest with it. This is hard for most people because we are trained to go...go...go....

Once you get caught in the flow, life just seems to move through and around you with ease. It seems as though a point is reached where no words are necessary to ask God or Universe for anything for it will already be provided to you as you are in the flow. The only thing left to do is not trying to stop the flow and getting out of it, which sometimes may be more difficult then we think. Being in the flow of life is to allow things to be as they are. Not trying to alter them to suit your needs or the needs of anyone else. Simply watching things happen and be as they are happening and being.

The rivers and rocks flow well together. Sometimes it looks like a rock is in the way of the water and interrupts the flow. That cannot be. Even the interruption of a rock is part of the natural flow and as long we allow the natural flow to occur as it was meant to, the water will find a way.

Bellingrath Gardens and Home, Theodore, Alabama.
Being in the flow is effortless and without struggle.

Bellingrath Gardens and Home, Theodore, Alabama.
Once you are in the flow it's hard to turn back but you can tread water for a while before going forward or simply be still in the flow.

OPPOSITE & ABOVE: McKinney Falls State Park, Austin, Texas.

It may take time to trust the flow of life and allow yourself to move freely without struggle. It's hard letting go of the illusory control of life we think we have, and sometimes we try to control. Eventually, though, we give up and go down the funnel.

Grand Canyon, Arizona.
A simple flowing river can move mountains.

Chinese Garden of Friendship, Sydney, Australia.
Photography by Jeff Allen.

Pelican Rock, City of Rocks State Park, Deming, New Mexico.

Rock

I wanna Rock! Rock! Den den a den, Den Den…
Not that kind of rock!

Meditating next to rocks reminded me of a game we used to play called freeze dance. When the music stops playing, you stop moving, simple enough? Although many of us cannot seem to sit still too long, as we are conditioned to always be on the go and be on the lookout for the next thing we need to do or be involved in. These rocks, however, have been in the same place for years. Even the little rocks outside your home are in the same spot unless you move them.

Belleville, Illinois.
The National Shrine of Our Lady of the Snows.

City of Rocks State Park, Deming, New Mexico.

We loved waking up to this beautiful scene and meditating with the sunrise. The soft glow brought an even more aware stillness to the moment, and there was a natural calmness and harmony that seemed to be vibrating from the rocks.

Cathedral Rock (basin), Sedona, Arizona.
These rocks seem to call out to be placed in sculpture form and the hikers comply.

These huge boulders in Arizona have been in the same spot unmoved watching the passersby. The energy of the rocks is so alive with the warmth of the sun and the coolness of the moon. The rocks are the perfect teaching tools to just stop…stop everything and look around and see where you are headed and in fact if you are headed in the right direction. Many times that stopping point is the most difficult thing to do. We are all caught in the flow of life and movement of it all. Yet, once we stop, we can make a conscious choice whether we want to rejoin the flow or pick up a road less traveled, neither being an easier way to be. Although, the stopping point within time is a joyful place to rest.

Being in nature and sitting on a rock is such a wonderful experience. There is so much to be learned from nature and rocks. Hopefully this book will encourage you to go out into nature and learn for yourself the beautiful lessons it has to offer you.

Coral Castle, Homestead, Florida.

Coral Castle, Homestead, Florida.
Much like City of Rocks State Park and the red rocks of Sedona, Arizona, there is an energy that seems to permeate from the area.

Coral Castle, Homestead, Florida.
One of world's greatest wonders, Edward Leed Skalnin built Coral Castle from 1923 to 1951. Yet, to this day, like the pyramids, scientists cannot figure out how he did so.

The Dawes Arboretum, Newark, Ohio.
Why are some people called to move and place rocks in a certain way? Have the rocks been speaking to us all of these years and some have the ears to hear them?

The Dawes Arboretum, Newark, Ohio.
The red Japanese maple rests amonq the rocks.

Water

While at a church service not too long ago a number of my own fears were brought to the surface. The next day it rained and rained. The rain made me think of a friend who had once interpreted a dream of mine as a clearing of emotions because I was walking through a storm. Somehow that worked for me — the rain outside my window was seen as a clearing of my emotions.

In many cultures, water represents the emotional baggage related to ourselves and our family. When we have awareness at our side and can easily recognize what is happening, it is easier to go through some of the emotional hiccups. Next time it rains or you are near water or you dream about water, ask yourself, "Where in my life am I doing some emotional clearing?" You may be surprised at what comes up. Relax and let the water wash away the debris in your mind.

Hollywood Beach, Florida.
One can notice the power of water by simply watching the waves of the ocean.

Japanese Tea Garden, Golden Gate Park, San Francisco, California.
Photography by Jeff Allen.

ABOVE & RIGHT: Bellingrath Gardens and Home, Theodore, Alabama.
Think about how we are interconnected with and dependent on water for our survival. Sometimes our emotional state may be reflected in the water. They can be turbulent like a stormy ocean or gentle like a stream.

McKinney Falls State Park, Austin, Texas.
Do something nice for someone or the environment and notice the ripple effect.

Ormond Beach, Florida.
We all leave wakes and ripple of energy. We can make a conscious decision whether we make positive or negative ripples.

Collingswood, New Jersey.
Water has the flow and power to move around any and all obstacles. Can we allow our minds to become water like?

Oglebay Park, Wheeling, West Virginia.
Open yourself to love.

The Dawes Arboretum, Newark, Ohio.
Open yourself to wherever the flow may take you...

There is always a way out no matter how hard life seems.

OPENINGS

My favorite line from the movie "The Sound of Music" is: "When God closes a door somewhere he opens a window." A friend of mine recently lost her job and, in the chaos of the aftermath, is trying to look for that open window. It is definitely a difficult view to keep when you are going through a trying time. Yet these are the times upon which we grow the most and are placed on the right spiritual path. It is easy to look in hindsight and recognize these trying moments as growing experiences, but as we're going through them it is hard to view. If we can just remember this small saying and know there is a window open for us somewhere, we can get through the experience with a larger awareness and a lot less suffering.

In the accompanying images, these openings are a reminder to keep your mind open and trust the process — the process in which you will be taken care of and that you will not be let down by god. Stay on the journey and be still and know. Listen to the silence and the voice within to guide you toward that open window.

St. John Neumann R.C. Church, Mount Laurel, New Jersey.
Open to forgiveness of yourself and others.

Christchurch, The Garden City, New Zealand.
There is a small opening in this tree…and this (opposite page) is what you find when you walk through it. *Photography by Jeff Allen.*

Stages of Development

CHAPTER FOUR

OPPOSITE & ABOVE: Bellingrath Gardens and Home, Theodore, Alabama.
Life is always present. One just has to be aware of it and the interconnection of living things.

LIFE

One of the first things we noticed in our journey across the country was life in nature and the beauty of the wildlife in the landscapes and gardens we visited. We began to realize that the birds, frogs, and other animals don't care about jobs, houses, cars, and titles. They *experience* life. We as humans forget often that life is about living. It's about our experiences, not how much money you make or how much you work. It's not all about your house, car, and possessions. It's about simply living and experiencing. When you begin to free your mind of the human conditioning and all of the human drama, a whole new world opens up. Spend time in your garden or a park near you and the wildlife will show you this. Birds are not worried or stressed out about your house or your government. They are busy living life. It seems most morning birds wake up and sing as the sun rises. It would be a different world if humans did this as well. You could even say that animals have a natural way of loving life. How many people can say the same? Maybe we should take a cue from the animals.

Bellingrath Gardens and Home, Theodore, Alabama.
Two turtles greeting the sunlight.

Everglades, Florida.
This guy is alive! He enjoyed having his picture taken. So we think…

Flagler County River to Sea Preserve, Flagler, Florida. The swarm is munching.

McKinney Falls State Park, Austin, Texas.
Life is beautiful... Notice how delicate and intricate the spiders web is and the dew drops on her back.

Blue Springs State Park, Florida.
Maybe looking for a fish to connect with?

Taos, New Mexico. This dog has seen it all.

DEATH

Another type of landscape we were led to in our journey was graveyards. Sitting in a graveyard, the topic of death naturally comes to mind. Death is a natural part of the cycle of the life of the body, but it's not something everyone is comfortable with. As you look at these pictures, do they bring up a fear of death in you? If you have a fear of death, it may be something you want to face. By facing the fear and overcoming it, you can live life more fully here in the present moment. Fear of any kind distorts our view of life.

Haddonfield Baptist Cemetery, Haddonfield, New Jersey.
Sit down. Relax. Experience the stillness of the moment.

Haddonfield Baptist Cemetery, Haddonfield, New Jersey.
Founded in 1818, as this cemetery shows, beauty and peace are everywhere when one has the eyes to see. Meditating in a cemetery can also help ease the fear of death.

Go sit at a graveyard near you. Just relax and meditate and see if you can calm yourself in the presence of death. Look for the still part in you that does not die with the body and allow yourself time to experience that stillness. Let yourself relax and be fine with nature and the natural cycle of life. As you release your fear, you also release stress. Then healing can naturally occur from the space you have created by releasing that fear. The spiritual practice of meditating in graveyards or even with dead bodies has been around for hundreds, if not thousands, of years, though it has not been accepted in our culture that much because of our materialistic view of life. We view the body as if it is who we are and act as if it's our greatest possession. We rarely realize that we are the spirit in the body and *not* the body itself. The body is a wonderful tool and temple, but it is not who we are. This practice of relaxing in a graveyard around death may help you experience this realization for yourself.

ABOVE: On the Road in Arizona.
Dusk in Arizona, the death of another day.

Sea Skeletons, Flagler County River to Sea Preserve,
Flagler, Florida.

LEFT & ABOVE: Open Fields, Lititz, Pennsylvania.
Without death there is no rebirth. Change is the only constant.

Christchurch, The Garden City, New Zealand.
This beautiful flower is death for a fly. *Photography by Jeff Allen.*

REBIRTH

When these lava fields erupted, it left the earth burned and dead for miles. It is amazing to see that out of that death there is such a beautiful rebirth once again showing the ever-changing natural cycles of life. Today these lava fields that were dead years ago are filled with abundant life. Trees and animals thrive once again. Relaxing and contemplating this may help you understand the concepts of life, death, and rebirth. You can almost say there is only life. Life continues to find a way. Look into life and what you will find is awareness and natural intelligence. This is who you are. You are awareness. You are the intelligence that allows the universe to exist in the first place. Perhaps we can say there is no birth and that death or rebirth just changes in one's awareness, or we can say there is just life and that is who you are and always have been. Allow yourself to relax with the idea above. Maybe play with it and explore it. You don't have to agree with the writings in this book, but if you explore the ideas you will expand your awareness. Your consciousness and presence will grow by letting yourself out of the conditioned box most of us live in and explore. The more you question and explore in meditation, the more "rebirths" you will experience in this life you are living right now.

Sunset Crater Volcano, Arizona.
New life ascends from a lava field, as the destructive ash revitalizes and fertilizes the land for new growth to come.

Sunset Crater Volcano, Arizona
We may look at a volcanic eruption as a negative event, but some plants and organisms thrive in the aftermath.

Ormond Beach, Florida.
Everyday the flower is reborn.

Blue Ridge section of Appalachian Mountains, Virginia.
Green leaves filling in the trees in spring.

MOON

Gazing at the moon can be a great experience. Go outside and find a place to sit or lie down and simply gaze at the moon. Do not have any preconceived ideas about the moon and do not analyze her. Just simply be with the moon and experience it. As you relax you may find yourself experience an energy field or a connection to between yourself and the moon that you may have never felt before. Relax into this. Gaze at the moon like a lover and rest in all of her beauty.

Ormond Beach, Florida.
We enjoy the simplicity and the space of this photograph

City of Rocks State Park, Deming, New Mexico.
The moonlight seems to soften the landscape.

City of Rocks State Park, Deming, New Mexico

The moon seems to fade as the sun rises. Is the moon fading or is the sun rising?

Sedona, Arizona.

While taking this shot lots of people walked by and I was becoming annoyed. I realized and watched my annoyance and slowly it faded.

Cathedral Rock, Sedona, Arizona.

SUN

Sun Gazing is an ancient practice that is once again resurfacing. It is an interesting and powerful practice in my opinion; however, we are not going to delve deeply into it here. If you do have an interest in sun gazing, we recommend checking out Hira Ratan Manek (HRM) for some guidelines. You can find out about his teachings at www.youtube.com or www.solarhealing.com.

Washington Oaks Gardens State Park, Palm Coast, Florida.
The sun feeds the rose and the rose reflects its brilliance.

If you are going to try sun gazing, please be safe and cautious. Only do what feels right to you and remember that any guidelines or rules given by someone are not always going to be perfect for you every time. So always allow yourself leeway to modify any practice to meet your own personal needs. We are all individuals and we all have different requirements, so always listen to and trust your intuition.

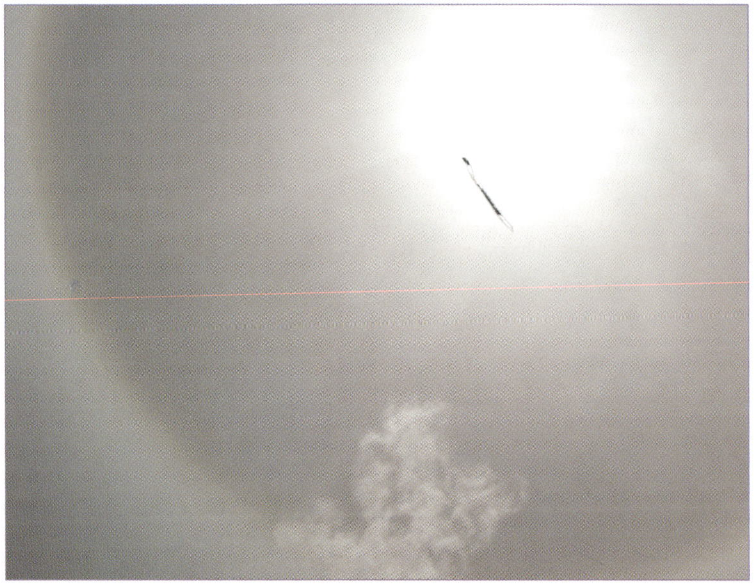

ABOVE & RIGHT: Ormond Beach, Florida.
This is not a camera effect or an illusion. This rainbow was around the sun for two days.

Ormond Beach, Florida.
The sun is a great role model. It gives generously without asking for anything in return. It is true unconditional love, so relax and become one with it.

Cellular Sun Meditation

This meditation, if practiced often and sincerely, can change your life and the environment around you.

1. Sit down in a comfortable position; close your eyes and allow yourself to become as relaxed as you can. Take a few moments to calm yourself.

2. Sense the cells in your body. Do your cells have borders? Are they solid? Let your cells shine like stars, allowing the life inside the cell to shine out into the world for a few minutes. When you are ready, the borders of the cells can be lost.

3. Allow yourself to become a ball of light like the sun, shining life from the inside of your body out into the world. As this light shines, it evaporates the pains in the body and any sadness, anger, or stress you're feeling. Let yourself rest in this place of peace, letting your inner light shine bright out into the world.

Final Meditations

CHAPTER FIVE

Washington Oaks Gardens State Park, Palm Coast, Florida.
Tai Chi will help your full potential blossom.

TAI CHI MOVING MEDITATION

Doing Tai Chi in different environments is a good way to find your center. Different natural areas will produce varied results, but still challenge you with a variety of energies. For instance, when doing Tai Chi on a windy day, you can feel the resistance of the wind and your body's struggle to keep the proper form of each move, but when doing Tai Chi on a beautiful sunny day, there is no struggle and the moves flow easily and effortlessly.

Tai Chi is a beautiful moving meditation that results in calming the body and mind and regrouping your spirit for challenges ahead. It is also great to do anywhere: a garden setting, parking lot, a mountain, or by the beach — anywhere and anytime that you are feeling overwhelmed or you just need to center yourself.

OPPOSITE: Gap, Pennsylvania.
Tai Chi can be done anywhere, including in this field of dandelions.

Washington Oaks Gardens State Park, Palm Coast, Florida.
Tai Chi is helpful in moving stuck or stagnant energy in the body that can cause illness.

Christchurch, The Garden City, New Zealand.
Photography by Jeff Allen.

Somewhere in West Virginia.
Tai Chi is meditation in motion. One becomes like a river, moving around obstacles with ease and grace.

Appalachian Mountains, Tennessee.
The flow of Tai Chi may help one enter the flow of life

WINDHORSE MEDITATION

All meditations are tools to get you from one point to the next. The windhorse meditation may work for a while, then you may find you have to abandon it for a time — only to come back to it at a later date. That's okay! Just like your garden changes the flowers it grows depending on the season, so too will the meditations you find needed. In times of uncertainty, though, when you're faced with the decision to go either left or right, the windhorse meditation is helpful to keep you moving on the right track. This meditation is called upon to bring about smoother pathways.

Chinese Garden of Friendship, Sydney, Australia.
Photography by Jeff Allen.

North Western New Mexico. The Windhorse Meditation like all meditation techniques may be great at first but at some point you may outgrow it and need to let it go and move on.

St. John Neumann R.C. Church, Mount Laurel, New Jersey.
Try doing the Windhorse Meditation in a nearby park.

Hollywood Beach, Florida.
Sometimes the clouds move slow and sometimes fast. Change is inevitable no matter the speed.

Chinese Garden of Friendship, Sydney, Australia.
Photography by Jeff Allen.

1. With this particular meditation, it is helpful to lay down and close your eyes. Take several natural breaths and relax with the stillness of the room and your own body.

2. Now imagine your legs are the color orange from your feet to your hips and call upon the tiger. Feel what it must be like to be a tiger — the way a tiger moves, catches its prey, and cares for its family. Rest in this vision and lose yourself in the tiger. Keep breathing slowly and naturally and imagine your stomach and waist all the way up to your chest the color white.

3. Now you are calling upon the Lion. Imagine what it must be like to be a lion, taking care of its family and being the king of the jungle. See the way a lion moves. Rest in this vision and allow yourself to be at peace with it. Keep breathing slowly and naturally and as you move up imagine your chest and your arms and all the way up to your neck and shoulders the color red.

4. Now call on the power of the Guruda. Imagine what it must be like to be this beautiful bird soaring in the sky getting a perspective of a total view of your situation. Feel the wonder of the wind on your wings and clouds floating by you. Keep breathing slowly and naturally and move up to your neck and your head with the color blue.

5. Now call on the Dragon. Feel what it is like to be a dragon — rest in that feeling as you continue to breathe slowly and naturally. At the end of this mediation, call upon the windhorse and ask it to bring about smooth pathways and keep you on the correct path. your heart shine out love and peace in all directions to all of the beings. How does your heart feel? Stay with this visualization for a few more minutes and then relax quietly for a few minutes.

ROSE MEDITATION

THE ROSE IS IN THE TOES

(Accompanying images from Columbus Park of Roses, Columbus, Ohio.)

You walk with me in day and night
We go so far without a fright....
But now I'm feeling some pain and so blue
At the thought of losing you.

We've been together for so long
And you deserve much more then this poem
I know you keep getting worse and redder
But I would love to make you feel better

If the time comes where we must part ways
Know that I will long for days
Where we ran together as one and in happiness
Know I will miss you but I won't be in distress

Roses and branches sometimes part ways
And so do children and parents and nights
and days
So you and I shall learn to live apart
Although you will forever be in my heart!

Each rose had a different scent yet they were all equally enjoyable.

A rose garden is a great place to meditate upon your senses. Look and smell indiscriminately at the roses or flowers and be with the true experience of the moment.

Bellingrath Gardens and Home, Theodore, Alabama.
Deeply experience the essence of your surroundings.

The Meditation

This meditation can help clear your mind, refresh your body, and allow the energetic blocks in your body that cause stress and illness to dissolve.

1. Sit down in a relaxed position. Close your eyes and allow yourself to become as relaxed as you can.

2. Scan your body with your mind. Visualize flowers growing out of every part of your body. You can go through your body section by section visualizing this. Feel the flowers growing. Be very creative. *(Note: You can visualize any type of flower and the flowers can be as big or small as you like.)*

3. Feel the flowers' energy flowing out from the inside of your body and into the world. Feel this out-flowing of energy as the energy of peace and love. Let this loving energy restore and refresh your body, mind, and even the world around you.

Washington Oaks Gardens State Park, Palm Coast, Florida.
Allow your awareness to become soft like rose petals.

Ormond Beach, Florida.
It's important to have full awareness. Most people would be distracted by the beauty of the lotus and miss the puddle that filled one of the leaves in the picture.

City of Rocks State Park, Deming, New Mexico.

We are human beings not human doers. We often forget we are the stillness and presence behind the doing. Take some time each day and simply be still. Witness the working of your mind and it will show you all you need to know.

STILLNESS MEDITATION

When you relax and become calm, you can sense the stillness in and around everything. Resting in nature can help the awareness of stillness grow within you. It's easier to sense this stillness in a more natural environment, but the stillness is the underlying presence in every thing and event. Jesus said, "Be still and know." When you begin to sense your inner stillness, you are close to your true self.

Lincoln Trail State Park, Marshall, Illinois.
Some questions to meditate on: Who are you? Who or what is aware? Can you find the part of you that you call you?

North Western New Mexico.
Allow your struggles to come through. Do not wrestle with your thoughts or emotions whether they are positive or negative. Just rest in stillness and witness.

We call ourselves human beings, but "human doings" may be more appropriate. Most of us are uncomfortable resting in our inner stillness because we feel we always need to be doing something. We are conditioned to go get, buy, exercise, work, want, and to keep busy at all cost because if we are not busy we are worthless. This is not true. With this busy, nervous program running inside of us, telling us to go...go...go, you can see why stress is so widespread in our society. When you become still, you start to see that not only is it okay to be still, but it also allows you to see the conditioned programs that have been controlling you and your life — and you can choose to let them go because they are finally made aware of.

By becoming still, you will begin to touch the teachings in silence and begin to touch truth. May your journey into peace and stillness be blessed!

City of Rocks State Park, Deming, New Mexico.
By resting in stillness one's body and mind naturally tends to come back to balance.

Washington Oaks Gardens State Park, Palm Coast, Florida.
Getting to a still point can be a struggle at first. It takes patience and effort to experience the clarity that stillness provides.

Coral Castle, Homestead, Florida.
Meditation is never a competition. Keep your meditation open and free. Do not judge yourself as to whether you are doing it wrong or right, good or bad.

The Meditation

The stillness and silence we are talking about here is not a quiet place outside of your self. It is the inner stillness and silence and it is always with you, but just rarely noticed. When you begin to experience this inner stillness and silence, you will experience the inner peace that is always with you. This meditation will uncover the inner peace. The environment around you may seem to be loud crazy and stressful to an onlooker but if you have found your inner peace you will be calm among the seeming madness.

The stillness meditation may be the most important meditation of all. It will take you on the journey of finding your inner peace, love, silence and stillness. You will uncover the peace and stillness that is always inside of you yet unnoticed because it is covered by the noise of thinking. The deeper you go, the more your peaceful still foundation will be realized and you will have this peaceful still awareness to stand on to live a peaceful, loving, and stress-free life. You will be free from the mind chatter and conditioned reactions influencing all of your decisions... You will find out what freedom truly is.

1. Sit down in a comfortable position. Close your eyes and allow yourself to become as relaxed as you can. Take a few moments to calm yourself.

2. Become aware of the body's sensations, simply feel them without judgment. Allow the sensations to be free as they are. Do not try to change them. Just witness them objectively. You may notice tightness, restriction of energy, or pain. Do not try to change them or label them as bad. Allow yourself to experience them as they truly are. You may notice as you witness these things they will start to dissolve on their own. Most of the time when we witness stress or pain in our body we run from it by ignoring it or try to get rid of it by taking medicine. This does not allow the stress or pain to untie itself and release. By quietly witnessing the pain, stress, and tension throughout the body and allowing it to express itself without labeling it or trying to stop it in some way, you begin to give it a chance to untie and heal itself. The body wants to be balanced and given the chance it will naturally fall back into harmony after you have stopped running and become the quiet witness. So just observe your body's sensations for a few minutes without judgment and allow the body to express itself freely without your ideas on how it should express itself.

3. When the body is fairly relaxed, start witnessing the mind. Become a silent observer, not judging anything about how the mind is thinking or reacting. Do your best witnessing the mind. It becomes easier the more you practice this. As you hear the voice or voices of the mind, just listen without reacting. Listen quietly to what is going on in your head. You may be surprised as to how much noise you hear. Do not try to stop the noise and quiet the mind. Let the mind be as noisy as it wants. Just listen to what's going on. Most people believe they have to quiet the mind to meditate. You cannot quiet the mind. The mind in time will become quiet due to you listening to it. You and your mind will begin to realize all of the unnecessary thoughts of fear, anger and stress swirling around never noticed before. You may start to see how you have been conditioned to believe certain things. By listening to the mind without interfering with it you will see what is causing many if not all of the problems in your life. Do not take my word for it. This may not make sense to you, but you have to go in and do the work. Listen to your mind and allow it to express itself. Don't try to correct your thinking or engage with the voices in the head while you are meditating. You will become lost in the noise of the mind and lose your observing viewpoint if you engage in conversation with the thinking. Most of us are used to having conversations with the voice in the head and you may find yourself engaging with it in the beginning, but each time this happens, do not criticize yourself, just gently come back to the observer's view point. The more you do this, the more your mind will untie and free itself from years of untrained, wild, noisy thinking. If you do this often and sincerely you will notice your mind and body becoming healthier and healthier and your relationship with the people around you and your environment becoming healthier and happier also.

Sedona, Arizona.
It's wonderful to sit on Bell Rock and experience the stillness that it permeates.

Coral Castle, Homestead, Florida.
The mind is always clear and expansive. We tend to fill it up with useless excessive thinking.

Afterword

Bellingrath Gardens and Home, Theodore, Alabama.
Grasping and chasing after peace, bliss, and love during meditation will leave you unfulfilled and aggravated. Allow it to come forth and surface naturally.

Spirituality is a funny thing, and, I must say, I am caught in this funny thing called spirituality. As I was putting this book together I experienced many highs and lows regarding the project. One day I was eager to share meditation tools and the next I was ready to throw it all out the window. Why? What was making me act this was. Depression? Fear? I had no clue. I kept reading more and more books on how to better myself and loved what they had to say. There were many authors who pointed to the same thing and many that disagreed, challenged me to go beyond, beyond what? What was there that I was missing? I finally discovered that I was missing nothing. Nothing.

I believe that I was missing nothing. Spirituality just like any religion is a concept. I was caught and lost in this concept for a long time. Believing that spiritual people had to behave a certain way and be nice to everyone and rise above mundane daily challenges. This only led to disappointment and hurt. This was my trap. A trap I had to see and let go of. What I am pointing to is a time when you just stop. Stop believing everything and anything. Stop assuming people are different then what they are and stop adding a story about what something will be like or not. Life will be disappointing, that's just how it is. But you don't have to let it affect you.

OPPOSITE: Bellingrath Gardens and Home, Theodore, Alabama.
Once you find your gem inside do not forget to be compassionate to others who may not have found theirs yet.

Spirituality has been around for eons and has had many different names throughout history. The best thing you can do for yourself is not put it on a pedestal. Searching and trying to get somewhere when you are already where you need to be is a waste of time. Stopping and realizing that it is a waste of time is a major accomplishment. The stopping point may be the best thing you do for yourself. Give it a shot and see what comes of it.

So, as you read this book, pick and choose what feels best for you at that particular time. Realize that all of the suggestions are just that, suggestions. Use them when you feel comfortable and see how you feel. There is an odd sense of freedom when you realize you need nothing or no one for support. That is not to say you will not do spiritual practices, go to church or gatherings, but you will not depend on outside sources or things to complete you.

We truly hope this book inspires you to go out into nature, relax, and live and love freely.

Sedona, Arizona.
The awareness that you truly are is closer to you than your heart or hand is.

The Dawes Arboretum, Newark, Ohio.
It's good to remember that the words written in this book — or any book — are only pointing to something you must find. The reading of words will never make you self-realized.

On the Road in Kansas.
We loved the change we experienced in Kansas, from stormy weather to sunshine.

Japanese Tea Garden, Golden Gate Park, San Francisco, California.
Photography by Jeff Allen.

Washington Oaks Gardens State Park, Palm Coast, Florida.
Keep your meditation practice light.

Ormond Beach, Florida.
Awareness will help you grow as a person.

What is your question?
Who can give you the answer?
Life is only now

Less Identified
Time is no thing to become
Untrue subtleties

Coffin in the ground
Coffin in the sky with God
No more talking please

Haikus

A haiku is a Japanese poem of three unrhymed lines of five, seven, and five syllables respectively. As we drove across America, taking pictures for this book, we noticed haikus would come to us. We rarely listened to the radio and this became a form of entertainment for us. Haikus can be used as a tool for a contemplative meditation. Just read the haiku and then relax with it. Let it dissolve into you and see if a deeper meaning of the haiku reveals itself to you. Do not think about the haikus meaning. Allow your insight to give you a revelation. Here are a few haikus for you to try out. Have fun and enjoy!

Children die in war
When you put down your weapon
The violence will end

Five seven five a
Seeming limitation
Refines expression

Angel hole in fence
When she puts her head through it
The backyard brightens

Bellingrath Gardens and Home, Theodore, Alabama.
We exercise our bodies yet rarely try to help the mind. The more you meditate, healing of the body, mind, and spirit will naturally occur.

City of Rocks State Park, Deming, New Mexico.

Let your path unfold
Then you won't have to be told
The jewel you behold

I sit in silence
Anxiety takes me hold
Wish I could regroup

Nela Loves Haikus
She knew how to spell that word
Why am I counting?

City of Rocks State Park, Deming, New Mexico.
Any place is a good place to rest and reflect.

I have no regrets
I did not live a clean life
The past is not mine

Do you enjoy clouds?
Do you enjoy sunny days?
Or do you work hard?

City of Rocks State Park, Deming, New Mexico.
We became used to settling into bed at dusk and rising at sunrise not having the distractions we normally had at home.

OPPOSITE & ABOVE: Grand Canyon, Arizona.
We must lose our fears and let go of our greed and manipulative ways to have a world of peace and equality. To have peace and love in one's life one needs to be peaceful and loving.

Recommended
Readingings

OPPOSITE & ABOVE: Washington Oaks Gardens State Park, Palm Coast, Florida.
May all beings never be without genuine joy and be awake and aware during their journey.

These are some of our spiritual influences. We tried to diversify our list as much as we could because we realize every person has her or his own journey in life. Many flavors, one heart.

Appalachian Mountains, Tennessee.
May all beings be without suffering and the causes of suffering.

Teachers

These teachers have websites and books and can be found on Youtube.

Eckhart Tolle
Thich Nhat Hanh
Gangaji
Byron Katie
Louise L. Hay
Joel S. Goldsmith
Mooji
Adyanshanti
Gregg Braden

Books

Anthony, Robert. *The Ultimate Secrets of Total Self-Confidence: A Proven Formula That Has Worked for Thousands, Now It Can Work for You*. New York, New York and Garden City, New York: Morgan James Publishing, unabridged edition 2007.

Elkins, Don, James Allen McCarty, and Carla Rueckert. *The Ra Material: An Ancient Astronaut Speaks* (The Law of One Series). Virginia Beach, Virginia: Donning Company Publishers, illustrated edition 1984.

Gangaji. *Diamond In Your Pocket*. Boulder, Colorado: Sounds True, Inc., reprint edition 2007.

Goldsmith, Joel S. *Leave Your Nets*. Camarillo, California: Acropolis Books, first edition 1998.

The Art of Spiritual Healing. San Francisco, California: HarperOne, 1992.

Hay, Louise L. *You Can Heal Your Life*. Carlsbad, California and New York, New York: Hay House, Inc., gift edition 1999.

Katie, Byron and Stephen Mitchell. *Loving What Is: Four Questions That Can Change Your Life*. New York, New York: Three Rivers Press, 2003.

Pilgrim, Peace. *Peace Pilgrim: Her Life and Work in Her Own Words*. Santa Fe, New Mexico: Ocean Tree Books, 1992.

Rinpoche, Yongey Mingyur. *The Joy of Living: Unlocking the Secret and Science of Happiness*. New York, New York: Three Rivers Press, 2008.

Ruiz, Miguel. *The Mastery of Love: A Practical Guide to the Art of Relationship*. San Rafael, California: Amber-Allen Publishing, gift edition 2002.

Schucman, Dr. Helen. *A Course in Miracles*. New York, New York: Foundation for Inner Peace, 2007.

Shanti Christo Foundation. *The Way of Mastery*. Ashland, Oregon: Shanti Christo Foundation, 2004.

Tolle, Eckhart. *A New Earth*. Westminster, London: Penguin, reprint edition 2008.

The Power of Now: A Guide to Spiritual Enlightenment. Novato, California: New World Library, 2004.